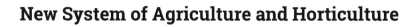

New System of Agriculture and Horticulture

NEW SYSTEM

OF

Agriculture and Horticulture.

A TREATISE

ON THE

FAILURE OF CROPS,

THE

DECLINE AND DECAY OF ORCHARDS,

THE CAUSES THEREOF AND THE REMEDIES THEREFOR,

Founded upon Fifty Years of Experience and Experiments by the writer,

DARIUS PEIRCE,

LIMA, WASHTENAW COUNTY, MICHIGAN

(Post-Office address, Chelsea, Mich.)

DETROIT:

TRIBUNE JOB OFFICE.

1869.

NEW SYSTEM

OF

𝕬𝖌𝖗𝖎𝖈𝖚𝖑𝖙𝖚𝖗𝖊 𝖆𝖓𝖉 𝕳𝖔𝖗𝖙𝖎𝖈𝖚𝖑𝖙𝖚𝖗𝖊.

A TREATISE

ON THE

FAILURE OF CROPS,

THE

DECLINE AND DECAY OF ORCHARDS,

THE CAUSES THEREOF AND THE REMEDIES THEREFOR

Founded upon Fifty Years of Experience and Experiments by the writer,

DARIUS PEIRCE,

LIMA, WASHTENAW COUNTY, MICHIGAN

(Post-Office address, Chelsea, Mich.)

DETROIT

TRIBUNE JOB OFFICE

1869.

PREFACE.

————•————

It is hardly necessary for the author of this work to make any excuses for its publication, since, notwithstanding the multiplicity of books and writings on Agriculture, Horticulture, and Pomology, there is none which seems to touch the subject for which this is designed

The elementary principles laid down in this work, are nothing more than the expression of facts, which experiments, investigation, and experience have developed, and while it will present to the producer, a system highly curious, and a subject of great practical interest, it will lead the naturalist to believe that the laws of Nature,˙ are equally inherent and efficient in a growing fruit tree and other vegetation, as they are in the production, growth, and habitudes of the different species of animals

The moral philosopher will see at once that nothing has been formed, through the fortuitous concurrence of circumstances, but that the whole vegetable kingdom bears the impress of creative agency and design. that the laws of Nature are as peculiar and distinctive in their formation of leaves, and blossoms, and fruits, as they are in any race of animals that traverse the earth's surface

3

INTRODUCTION.

———•••———

Farmers, this work now offered is not a servile compilation from other writings, but a simple, plain system, drawn together from numerous sources, and submitted to tests, and trials, and experiments by the author, for years, and he thinks he knows whereof he writes. This system presents to you a law of Nature, wherein the seed is the seat of life of the whole vegetable kingdom. This seed furnishes natural roots which are the natural feeders of all trees or plants This natural law carries with it its own natural penalties A law without a penalty, becomes a mere rule, and is no law; hence, Nature becomes the human teacher in making laws. An example of great magnitude, will be found in the cereal grains The seed when placed where Nature would place it, near the surface, spreads, grows, and forms a large green plant Another seed, covered deep, will not produce a plant at all, but will show two slim, long leaves. Both seeds possess equal fecundity and are equally prolific, yet the former will show from five to ten tall, full-grown straws with large heads, while the latter will show but one short, slim straw, with a dwarfed, short, green head. (In the former I have barely placed the common yield) Without stopping to present to the reader any suggestions relating to the penalties, or of submitting any mathematical calculation, the writer would simply inquire, how would this statement, if founded on facts, affect the granery of the world ? This work informs the grain grower, and reveals the astounding facts, that one-

5

third of the seed of the cereal grains sown, produces three-fourths of all crops now annually raised under our present system of cultivation. In this work the facts are made easy of solution, and the remedy simple and plain.

Having spun out this introduction to an inexcusable length, and having given much of the space contained in this work to orchards and fruit trees, the writer will close this offering with the single regret, that a subject of such vast importance to the people, had not found an abler advo-cate—one whose perceptive powers were less clouded by age, one whose sight was less bedimmed by time; and, finally, one who could write with a more pointed pen.

CHAPTER 1.

———◆———

SEC. 1.—The evidence that there exists certain natural laws which govern the growth, the form, the size, the shape, the health, and the strength of the whole vegetable kingdom seems to be conclusive.

SEC 2 —That these natural laws are fixed and cannot be altered, amended, or repealed, and when obstructed or violated will frequently produce the most dire calamities to such vegetables as these violations happen to fall upon, or are applied.

SEC 3 —By this law of Nature, all seeds were to fall on the surface of the earth, and there to sprout, vegetate, grow, and produce again

SEC 4 —By this law the seat of life would seem to exist right where the seed sprouted, right where the roots and body join, right where the heart terminates, right where the hollow in the straw ends, right where the pith ceases, right where the roots start down, right where the body, stem, stalk, or straw starts up, this being the place from which the sap is distributed through the arteries of the tree or plant

SEC 5 —The seed being the seat of life, the roots are the feeders, the body, stem, stalk, or straw are the things fed, while during the vegetating process the seed feeds both root and body.

VIOLATIONS—CEREAL GRAINS.

SEC. 6 —Nearly all seeds put into the earth, are sowed or planted in total disregard of these natural laws, but as these laws were not known, the consequences were not seen, and the penalties have remained unfelt

Sec 7—No seed permanently buried in the ground, so that it cannot spread immediately at the surface of the earth, ever did or ever will produce but one short, slim straw, with a dwarfed, short, green head This appears to be one of Nature's laws, and applies to all the small grains alike, or nearly so

Sec 8—We have "practiced a system of the most outrageous violations upon our apple orchards, and fruit trees generally ; and the violations differ as the trees and other vegetables are different, one from an other, and the calamities differ accordingly.

Sec 9 —All seeds produce one tier of roots and no more and it becomes absolutely necessary, that these roots should grow large, being the entire feeders of the tree or plant. Note •—In all these violations the plant and tree show a second tier of roots, or underground suckers, which come out of the body of the tree or plant, and not from the seed, and are illegitimate, unnatural, artificial, and destructive.

Sec 10—In order to make them grow large, the seed should be placed where Nature's law would place it, near the surface of the ground, where the heat, the light, the rains, the dews, will have an immediate effect upon the seeds while vegetating, and the subsequent growth of roots

Sec 11—All other roots growing out of the body, stem, stock, or straw, are not legitimate roots, but artificial, unnatural and mere suckers, which come out of the body of the tree or plant above the seat of life, and consequently furnish no nutriment for the whole tree or plant.

Sec. 12 —These artificial roots or suckers are produced in two ways, the one by burying the seed too deep, the other by banking the earth around the body, stem, stock or straw

Sec 13—No healthy or thrifty plant or tree can be found which possesses these artificial roots or suckers ; but, as

2

they will not grow without earth to grow into, it is difficult to determine whether the banking or the roots are most destructive.

SEC 14.—Cover the seat of life of any tree permanently with earth. and the leaves will turn yellow, dwindle in size, and the tree will either die, or produce these suckers, and the main roots below will decay and dwindle and will not grow.

CHAPTER 2.

—--- •••----

EXPERIMENTS AND DEDUCTIONS.

SEC. 1.—Take any tree, while the sap flows freely, cut or break a root, and let the tree stand a few weeks, then pull it up and split it, commencing at the root so cut or broken, and following the grains of wood, it will lead you to the end of one or more limbs, and you will find a black streak the whole length of root, body and limb or limbs, caused by the cut or break.

SEC 2—Take any fruit tree, small size for convenience, dig down and find any permanent root, cut or break it, and it will show the same black streak. The longer it stands the darker and plainer the black streak will be, until it becomes a black streak of rotten wood, the whole length of root, body and limbs.

SEC. 3.—Go into a forest of timber, cut a root off the tallest tree, and its destructive effect will be seen very soon by the dead limbs in the top of the tree.

EXPERIMENT NO 1.

SEC. 4.—In the year 1833, I set an orchard of 50 apple trees On account of the location of the Michigan Central Railroad, I removed them seven or eight years after. The trees had grown rapidly, and in removing I broke many large roots It could not well have been avoided I took great care in resetting, dug deep and large holes, manured with fine manure, finished setting according to Hoyle, and they all leaved and lived, and stood right there for 15 or more years, but did not grow—blossomed occasionally every other year. Some trees became entirely barren, and for years showed no blossoms. I grew uneasy. They did not look thrifty. I scoured with ashes and water, I grafted, pruned, examined and investigated. The apples became dwarfed knurly and wormy, the wood-lice covered the most of the trees, dead wood appeared in spots on southwest side of the body, dead limbs were plenty and mossy. I looked the Agricultural papers over, I tried ashes and chip-manure, I read of grub worms, of beetles, of borers, &c. One man said or seemed to say, I must punch the worms in their holes with a gimlet, and then hook their remains out with a crooked wire. But I found more holes in one tree than I could count.

THE CAUSE.

SEC. 5.—Some twelve or fifteen years since, I dug down and found the true origin and cause of the distress and destruction of my trees. In digging I chanced to light upon the end of one of those broken roots, (broken at the time of removal.) On splitting this root, I found nothing but a green shell of wood. I traced this rotten root and split it through root, body, and limbs and found the whole tree to contain a rotten mass of decomposed wood, covered by a thin shell of green wood, like a sugar coated pill.

SEC. 6.—I soon commenced and dug out all my trees, cutting and taking out armfulls of these knurly, curly roots or suckers. I found all the trees with four or five exceptions in the same condition of the one described. I dug all the trees out down to the main roots, carefully cutting all roots above, and left the earth in a ring around each tree at a distance of four feet, exposed the seat of life to the light and the heat, cleaned out the earth that was wedged between the main roots where they joined the body, exposed the tops of the main roots, and swept them clean two and a half feet from the tree the first season. The next spring I removed the earth to the distance of four or five feet.

SEC. 7.—All my trees were not alike. I found some more advanced in decomposition than others. Some two or three have cracked open, exposing the rotten wood the whole length of root, body and limbs. Others have enclosed the rotten wood with a solid body of green wood from five to eight inches in thickness. From a number of trees the rotten wood seems to be badly squeezed. Escaping juice of the rotten wood finds vent in cracks or seams, if, indeed, the pressure does not open these seams.

SEC 8—The question concerning the breaking of roots being the sole cause of the rotten wood contained in the trees is placed beyond the possibility of doubt to my mind. And numerous others, who have been engaged for years in experimenting on the same subject, entertain no doubts of its truths

SEC 9—The effect of the foregoing experiment has resulted in entire success. In digging around my trees, I found the roots in all shapes. Most of the main roots had grown up towards the surface of the ground, at the seat of life, or where the roots joined the body. I found every species of living creeping insects nestling in the mouldy, milldewed, slippery, slimy mass of decomposed wood.

SEC. 10.—Some roots not larger than my thumb when dug out were as large as my arm in the fall At the seat of life the body and roots spread out, and seemed to double in size the first summer, the trees took new life, the leaves changed color in four weeks and doubled in size, becoming a dark green The old bark started, the moss rolled off, the wood lice moved and fell from many trees the first summer.

Sec. 11—The most singular part of the whole remains untold, viz. that each and every tree that has lived, has blossomed and borne fruit without deviation every year, and nearly alike Since they were dug out, there is no every-other-year tree in this orchard , then large roots extend a great distance, and they resemble the great platform the forest tree stands upon. No plowing has ever been done in this orchard since the trees were first set out.

EXPERIMENT NO ²

Some fifteen years since, I sowed the seed, raised the plants and set an Osage orange hedge

A pamphlet giving directions accompanied the seed. This pamphlet informed me that I must pull up the trees at one year old, and cut off the roots to the length of just ten inches, and then set in rows. I followed directions, setting half a mile or more In order to make the hedge thicker I bent them down, and with hooks driven into the ground fastened in them. In the process of bending, they would break and split, and on discovering a black streak at the heart, I split a number of them, and in every case traced the black streak to the place where the root was cut at the time of setting

EXPERIMENT NO. 3.

Nearly thirty years ago, I set an orchard of seventy-five pear trees, plowed deep, manured heavy, grafted and budded, kept it in high state of cultivation, kept on manuring and plowing. In ten years from setting, one-fourth were rotten, in fifteen years one-half were rotten, so that they could not stand, and nearly half had fallen, and the rest are not worth curing And all this has come from the black streaks made by breaking roots with the plow

EXPERIMENT NO 4

In cutting a limb I cannot make the black streak run down at all. In grafting for the last fifteen or more years, I have tried hundreds of experiments, but in no case have I succeeded in making a rotten streak of wood run down the tree In girdling, the whole tree will die, the top first In climbing part way up a tree and then girdling it the leaves will all wilt above the girdle, but none below.

EXPERIMENT NO 5

In removing the earth from the basement for a barn, I covered the roots of a grove of shade trees, some six inches, some a foot or more, with earth. In two years there was not a live tree nor a green leaf on one of the trees, nor was there a single artificial root or sucker to be found. This grove was composed of white oak, yellow oak, sassafras and hickory.

GENERAL REMARKS

These experiments have been prosecuted by the author, for a number of years, and it would be impossible for him to condense and describe a tenth part of his investigations, and the conclusions he has arrived at.

Gentle reader, grant leisure to the imagination, and scan the vast field before you, the orchards of the continent, and perhaps of the world, and ask yourself the question, how many orchards there are that have never been plowed, and how many trees there are that do not possess these same black streaks, or the rotten body emanating from this cause alone. Gentle reader, if these statements made contain the elementary principles of truth, then the facts and conclusions that the apple orchards of America are and must be nearly all a rotten mass of decomposed wood, soul and body, root and branch, cannot be doubted nor questioned, when we reflect and take into consideration the facts, that the orchards have been plowed frequently, if not annually, and the roots of the trees are not only broken and torn from their moorings, the seat of life of the tree, but, they are cut into short pieces and turned bottom up, according to the science of Agriculture And this is not all, the back furrows are turned against and around the body of the tree, burying the stumps of the broken roots, and causing the second tier of roots to grow This same doctrine of breaking roots is the doctrine recommended, advocated and applied by the great mass of Agriculturalists, throughout the States of the Union, and a standing lesson for the students of the Agricultural colleges of many states.

CHAPTER 3.

————•————

VIOLATIONS, ETC.

[NOTE :—The reader will soon discover the vast field before him, and the magnitude of the subject contained in this chapter.]

SEC 1—By a law of Nature, the wheat kernel falls on the surface of the ground, and when placed there, or with a slight covering, barely sufficient to protect the seed, it will frequently spread out and form a large green plant or platform, from which I have counted, 20, 30, 60, 70, and sometimes 100 full grown straws with large heads and each coming from one kernel

VIOLATIONS

SEC. 2—No kernel of wheat, permanently buried, ever did, or ever will, produce but one straw—and a short, slim, slender straw, and a short, dwarfed green head.

SEC 3—No kernel of wheat buried or covered so that in the vegetating process it cannot spread right at the kernel, and spread on the surface of the ground, ever did, or ever will, produce but one slim, sickly, stunted straw, and a short green head.

SEC 4—This same law applies to all the small grains alike, or nearly so, and affects the corn crops very materially in their products, and, while the author of this work excludes all root crops, yet, and still, the potato vine will grow longer and larger with the eye planted up   Try it!

SEC. 5.—In all these cases of burial of the grain, you will

find the violation accompained by the second tier of roots or suckers.

SEC 6 —The first sprout of a kernel of wheat is a root. From this first root-sprout, and close to the kernel, starts a round sprout   As this round sprout grows, it unrolls, and leaves make their appearance through the hollow of it.   All spreading out on the surface, presents to us the appearance of a large flat green plant.

SEC. 7 —No person will assume that this green plant should be buried, or, if the seed is buried, this green plant would grow at all   If the seed is buried, the hollow sprout does not unroll, and the first leaves at the kernel die, and two slim, narrow, long leaves, emanating from the centre of the round sprout, will make their appearance, at the surface of the ground , and when the straw is formed, there will be a joint in it, a little below the surface of the ground, and, from this joint, grows a tier of roots, and at the kernel, you will have another tier of roots, and both these tiers of roots, will be very short and fine roots ; presenting a good example of the truths laid down in Sec 9 and 10 of this work, Chapter 1.

HOW TO EXAMINE WHEAT, OATS, &c.

SEC. 8—Having examined and investigated this subject for fifteen or twenty years, I would recommend a large knife to the reader, and a pail of water.   Take these, go to any field, cut out and wash the roots at any season of the year, and in any field sown you will very soon discover the truths contained in the statements just written.

GENERAL REMARKS.

Perhaps there is no situation in which a person finds a subject so difficult to describe, as the one presented to the reader, from the fact of its simplicity, and the ease with which the truths can be ascertained.

Go into any field, and you can then and there find the short straw ; dig down, and see for yourself.   Go into any field at harvest, and you will see this slim, short straw, shaking from the butt of the bundle, and slobbering the field.

3

The writer of this has taken a knife and pail of water, and has cut out, taken out and washed the plant, in all it stages of growth, he has examined the roots from time to time for years, from the first appearance of the sprout to the time of harvest, and knows that no kernel of grain, buried so that the first root cannot move or roll the kernel, while vegetating, or the rains wash it out, ever did or ever will produce but one slim, stunted straw, with a short green head, later to ripen, remains green longer, and that nearly all our grain comes from the surface kernels. The person who will examine this subject, will see mines of wealth concealed under the thinnest of veils, and while all entreaties of the writer may be given to the winds, the principles laid down in this work, will live and some day flourish.

One of the most familiar questions of the day is, what share of grain sowed is buried two inches or more? The writer cannot answer. Many people lay it at one-half, some one-third, some more or less. The writer believes there is double the seed sown necessary. The careless, heedless manner of putting in crops is so common, that there is no guide or rule which will enable a person to form an opinion.

Let us go to the bottom of these destructive habits, and you will see the seed sower hurrying in his crops. His whole object is to bury his seed out of his sight, regardless of con-sequences. If he drills, you will find the lower kernels all in a row, with their roots twisted, curled and grown into a solid nest; if he sows broad cast, he draws his large heavy drag, burying his seed beneath the dirt of traditions, gathered from the antidiluvians, accompanied by numerous other transgres-sions of the laws of Nature and of Nature's God.

CHAPTER 4.

———•◆•———

CORN CROPS.

SEC 1—The producer of this grain will gain much information by planting a few kernels deep, and a like number near the surface of the ground If he will actually perform it, and not talk, and write, and then neglect doing it, he will see the shallow-planted corn come up first, grow faster, stalks larger, and with more joints in a stalk It will be ahead of the deep planted corn the whole season, grow taller, ripen earlier, produce larger ears, and the ears will be filled better—generally to the end

SEC 2.—The kind of Indian corn, known as dent corn, will depreciate in the latitude of Detroit and run out, or become more flinty and will lose its dent form In my experiments, all the difference between the different species I have noticed is, while the dent begins to harden or glaze next the cob, the yellow or flint begins to harden or glaze on the outside of the kernel

EXPERIMENT NO 1.

SEC. 3 —In the year 1855 or 1856, I planted a five-acre lot; it was the second crop I plowed once, dragged level, marked the land three and a half feet each way, by drawing a chain ; planted three and a half feet one way, and just double that, or near twenty inches, the other one-half the field, four kernels in a hill ; the other half three , no hill was covered thicker than a hoe blade in the field or, from an 8th to a 16th of an inch of earth was put on top of the seed.

The common rules of cultivation were not necessary in this field, no cultivating or plowing was done after planting; no horse ever entered the field; the writer with one hand, spent a day perhaps going through the corn, and pulling the weeds, which were few; the land was clean and very fertile; the seed planted was of the white dent variety.

Could an accurate account and description of the growth of this corn be given, I know it would be entirely incomprehensible to many people. I shall only enter a few notes touching the growth and yield.

I paid $2 per acre for cutting and shocking, and the person employed by laboring early and late received nearly fifty cents per day. Much of the corn stood eleven feet high, many stalks had eighteen joints in a stalk, and some were carried many miles as curiosities, and a bushel basket would have held every small and soft ear in the field, including all ears not filled to the end.

From one measured acre of land, the shocks numbered one hundred and sixty-seven, and each shock yielded or exceeded two bushels of ears of corn. The whole field must have yielded 160 bushels of shelled corn to the acre.

In an examination of the roots of this corn, many were traced 7 feet, and in no place did we find these roots to exceed two inches below the surface of the ground, while the ground appeared to be full of these long roots. So full was the ground of these large roots crossing and recrossing each other, that it seemed as though no horse could have drawn a cultivator through the field at this season of the year.

Reader, we all know and acknowledge the necessity and utility of destroying weeds in the corn, but great care should be observed in using the cultivator too late in the season. In the season following, I planted the same field in the same manner and obtained the same growth or larger, but a hurricane and hail storm damaged my crop.

TURNIPS.

In sowing turnips, drag level, sow seed, and drive a flock of sheep over the ground. I have tried it with success, but have never used the sheep's foot to other seed, but should like to see the experiment tried.

GENERAL REMARKS

All seeds placed in the ground will be affected by the elementary principles laid down in the first chapter of this work From what course has this theory of burying our seed come The acorn falls on the surface of the ground, the apple falls and rots on the surface of the ground, our grains all in a state of nature did the same Where did the theory of deep planting come from ? From habit ? If so, I ask, why has the science of agriculture no depth to recommend, no rule of depth to govern themselves in putting their seed into the ground ? They have no rule.

INSECTS

There is a doctrine published and proclaimed through the country and generally credited, believed and promulgated, that insects were created and formed for the purpose of attacking, eating, digesting, consuming and destroying sound trees, sound timber, sound wood, sound fruit trees, and the fruits thereof, sound blossoms, sound grains, either green or ripe, sound seed, either in the ground or on the ground, sound roots of trees, standing or lying, and that the whole vegetable world are barely suffered to exist and grow through the kind leniency of these in sectiverous, carniverous, gormandizing, destroying, flying, scenting, creeping, crawling smelling tribes.

The writer asks the poor privilege of dis-enting from the expressed and oft repeated views of gentlemen of high standing in this Agricultural, Horticultural world on this subject, and, feeling desirous of avoiding repetitions as far as possible, he will leave the reader to gather the views of the writer from other chapters.

NOTE —The writer believes and will insist on the doctrine, that sound trees will produce sound fruit, as a generally laid down principle, and that sound blossoms and sound plants are seldom attacked by insects ; that as a general thing we kill the tree or plant, and then the insect takes possession ; that a rotten-hearted tree will produce diseased fruit, and a deep covered seed will produce a diseased plant, &c.

CHAPTER 5.

Having developed, written, and in a partial manner demonstrated to the reader the existence of a law of nature, and several experiments all going to prove the same, and on taking a survey of the whole field the writer has arrived at the following conclusions, viz :

FIRST.—That a tree is a tree anywhere, and an apple tree forms no exception to the rule

SECOND —That the apple tree is an artificial tree, and its fruit is artificial, having been taken from its wild state; consequently, should be cultivated like other trees.

THIRD —That no tree can live and flourish unless its first main roots, where they join the body, are above the ground ; that a second tier of roots is death to any tree; and disease, disaster and destruction to all crops whose seeds fall on top of the ground in their natural state.

FOURTH —That no grubworm, beetle, borer, ant, catterpillar, curculio, or fly, or bug ever attacked, eat, entered or meddled with sound timber, sound trees, sound blossoms, or sound grains, or the plants thereof

FIFTH.—That plowing orchards causes three deaths—breaking roots, burying the seat of life, and causing the second tier of roots to grow ; that the three combined are slow death, but terrible, cruel, and sure

SEC 2.—Reader my first conclusion is before you. Can any person say an apple tree forms an exception to other trees? If it is a tree why not treat it like other trees ? History informs us that apple trees bore apples in the Garden of Eden.

Even Webster's dictionary, says our apple trees are supposed
to have originated from the English crab, that in its wild
state its roots grew on the surface of the earth the same as
a forest tree

SEC 3—My second conclusion consists in the changes
made, and mankind generally believe that any tree or plant
that will submit to a transfer from the forest to the open
field or garden, leaves its wild nature, and people call the
tree or plant thus removed "civilized" or "tamed" Usually,
they proceed to improve its fruit, its seed, as well as the plant,
o tree itself It is thus the apple tree stands, an artificial
Speaking, through this law of nature "You have improved
my fruits and made them grow large. I furnish you a large
variety of the most delicious fruits I once had roots that
fed and nourished my body In the woods my roots obtained
this nourishment from the rich surface ; now, I am not allowed
to grow roots nearer the surface than the plow runs" The
tree, thus speaking, falls back on the laws that governed
its origin, and speaks in a manner, not to be misunderstood :
" Give me roots, or eat worms !"

My third conclusion is that no tree can live and flourish
whose roots are not above the ground at the seat of life.
The above is one of the first principles laid down in this
work and a very important one The second clause speaks
of the second tier of roots, &c We have seen that the seed
should be on top of the ground, and we have seen that the seed is
the seat of life This places the main roots and seat of life
right where Nature's laws place all roots The tap root is not
a necessary feeder, not but what it furnishes some sort of
nourishment from the depths of the cold earth to which it
descends Still, it is evident from millions of mouths, attached
to the radicles of the surface roots, that the nutriment on
which the tree's existence depends comes from that source.

WHEAT, RYE, OATS, ETC

That there is more seed used than is necessary may be
seen and ascertained by examining Any kernel placed on

the surface of the ground will show a large green plant, with broad leaves, and will cover quite a space of ground, while the deeply covered seed will not produce a plant, but two slim, long leaves The truth is, we kill the seed before it lives; the difference between the kinds of covering given to the seed, is so marked, in all fields, as to preclude the necessity of even scrutiny If the seed is sown on the surface of the ground where your plants can spread, it becomes a large plant; it obtains health, strength, stability and size.

INSECTS

4th CONCLUSION.—While writing in experiment No 1, I spoke of finding every species of living, creeping insect It was here that I found the grubworm, the beetle, the borer, the ant, the curculio, and the caterpillar, in and around the bodies of the trees of numerous orchards I have had occasion to examine. I have usually found where the back-furrow had been piled around the body of the tree, year after year, their nests, their camping grounds, generally in and about the body I found a mouldy, mildewed, slippery, slimy, mass of decomposed wood, filled with these vipers, their camps, their fortifications, their tombs, their dead, their sepulchres, their old, their halt, their blind, their young, their eggs, their larvæ.

Reader, these insects are not guilty of such enormous crimes as is commonly laid to their charge They are a necessary evil, if indeed they are an evil at all These slandered insects were made, created, produced for the express purpose of devouring and destroying all the woody and animal carrion of the earth The offals of all putrid matter is their Eden, their home Search manure heaps, there you will find them In your barn yards they are plenty, your chip piles are filled with them, your rich soils always furnish an abundance of insects, your sickly, dying, decomposed, gangrene fruit trees, furnish, rear, and breed millions and myriads of these buzzing, flying, creeping, crawling diatribes

Reader, go into your wheat field There you will find the midge, the weevil, the Hessian fly, and a critical examination for facts, will disclose and confirm the truths before written.   You will find the short, slim, sickly, half-decomposed plant, and green heads, to be filled with these insects We hear great complaints all over the country , some complain of wire worms, some the grub worm Gentlemen, please dig down and see how deep your seed was covered ; see if the yellow leaves were not caused by a sickly plant

It is a fact that in all my examinations I find the midge, the wevil and the fly, in the short green heads first Then by the laws of increase and multiplication, starvation ensues. Then they will sweep every thing of the vegetable kind Examples of this kind are not uncommon in the West with the grasshopper .

THE PLOW.

FIFTH CONCLUSION —Reader, my two last conclusions are so intimately connected that I shall treat the subject as one Plowing orchards causes three deaths to trees, viz :

FIRST DEATH—Breaking roots is always followed by a black heart of rotten wood, the whole length of body, limbs and roots

SECOND DEATH—Piling the earth around the body of the tree, as laid down in Sec 10. of General Principles, 1st. Chapter ; also, see experiment number 5, 2d Chapter

THIRD DEATH—Causing a second tier of roots to grow by banking or turning the back furrow against and around the tree.

Reader, the root of a tree is its sheet anchor, its feeder. Can you feed a calf at any other place than its mouth ?   Is the root of a tree to be considered the root of all evil ?

Lo! the plowman enters the great American orchard, arrayed in all the paraphernalia made necessary for the occasion, with his team and his plow, his cutter, his jointer, and at once proceeds according to order He cuts all roots into short pieces and turns them bottom up in a scientific manner He piles the earth around the trees ; the black streaks which always follow the breaking of roots, run through the whole body and limbs of the tree ; the wood soon begins to decay and rots from bottom to top ; decomposed wood with all its attractions for insects follows ; the grubworm enters , the ant takes possession , the caterpillar seeks it ; the curculio follows in the wake of his predecessors The borer scents the woody carrion afar off. The atmosphere is infected, the blossom is tainted, the honey bee deserts it, the flies blow it, the maggot eats his way into the core of the apple, the people eat the apple, or drink the cider, and pick the skins from their teeth.

[NOTE :—The writer is not ignorant of the fact, that there are certain worms, like the cutworm, and other insects like the striped bug, and a class of caterpillars whose subsistence is the leaves of vegetables—like the silkworm, and perhaps other insects.]

CHAPTER 6.

———— • • ————

THE CURE FOR FRUIT TREES

Sec 1 —Enter your orchard at any time after the frost is out of the ground (in the spring of the year is the best time); remove the earth from and around the tree to the distance of three feet the first year, cut all small knurly roots clean from the body of the tree, remove turf, sprouts, and every thing down to the main roots, remove the earth wedged between the main roots and next to the body, leave the bottom of the main roots resting on the earth The seat of life is right where the main roots join the body , this should be exposed and made clean The second year remove the earth five or six feet from the body. I leave the earth in a ring, others do not, but cut it off

Sec 2 —Care should be taken to cover the same you exposed, the winter following the exposure The covering should be made before hard freezing, and should be removed in the spring following, and should not consist of straw on account of mice

Sec. 3 —The covering need not be repeated after the first year, the object being to prevent the freezing and cracking of the monstrous growth of new wood, which usually follows the process described above

Sec 4 —An example of this kind exists within one mile of the home of the writer of this work, and in the orchard of the Hon Rodney Ackley. The trees cracked from the freezing

SEC 5.—The reader must exercise judgment in the distance the roots should be exposed, as large and old trees will bear the removal farther than trees of smaller size In your proceedings council the laws of Nature. Examine the great platform the forest tree stands upon

GENERAL REMARKS.

SEC 6 —Reader, after you have relieved your trees from their burthens, please say unto them, "Thou mayest grow, and flourish in accordance with the laws of thy nature , I planted thee for the purpose of having thee to grow, I buried thy roots on purpose to have them to grow, therefore know ye I will never break thy roots more."

SEC. 7.—Please say unto the plow, "Thou hast done thy work thoroughly, thou hast been a faithful servant, thou hast cut all the roots of my fruit trees into short pieces, and turned them under in a scientific manner, thou hast not only plowed, but thou hast cross plowed these roots, thou hast piled the earth around my trees according to the rules and laws of agriculture to my entire satisfaction "

SEC 8 —"Therefore, in consideration of thy faithful services I give and grant leave of absence unto thee from my orchard forever In testimony hereof Mr. Harrow will ever stand as a swift witness. '

SEC 9 —Gentle reader, I would say to the insects throughout all the orchard, ' Thou hast multiplied excessively, thou hast fulfilled the mission for which thou wast created, thou hast scented, come hither, enjoyed and destroyed all the animal and vegetable carrion, in accordance with the laws of thy creation and tastes "

SEC. 10.—"Thou hast created a great commotion among the human family, nay, among the great men, causing them to be divided in their opinions concerning the purposes and intentions of thy creation."

SEC. 11 —"Whereas thou art accused of eating, attacking, gnawing, and boring, and destroying the fruit trees and the fruits thereof, throughout all the land, therefore I would say unto them, assemble thy forces, gather thy strength, and hold thy last universal and high carnival in consideration of the crimes thou hast committed, for there will be famine and hunger, and weeping, and wailing, and gnashing of teeth among thy different sects "

WHEAT, ETC —THE CURE FOR WHEAT AND A LL SMALL GRAINS

SEC. 12 —"Plow deep while sluggards sleep, and you shall have corn to sell and to keep," says Poor Richard. The remedy in this case consists entirely in the covering ; still, it is necessary that the field should be mellow down deep, as the roots are larger and run deeper when the kernel has but one set of roots, and those near the surface

SEC 13 —Remember the law of Nature, that all seeds produce but one tier of roots, and those roots placed near the surface of the ground, where they receive the immediate heat of the sun, the dews of the evening, and the warm showers of the morning ; and any and all other roots, do not come from the seed, but must come from the body, stock or straw, and are forced from the straw by the burying of the seed, and are artificial, unnatural, and destructive

SEC 14 —The covering should be very light, and as near- ly equal on the whole seed as it can be, and for that purpose the ground should be rolled before sowing, if sowed broad- cast ; then use a very light drag, with short teeth—two inches long is enough. Railroad spikes make good teeth

SEC. 15 —I trust the reader will bear with an experiment or two, as some backwoodsman may find an example that may be of service to him . Then, first, in all timbered lands it follows that in the first crops there is no plow used, and frequently not half the seed covered The wheat al- ways covers the stumps, with the tallest of wheat. The only reason I ever heard assigned was, it was " new land." I never was satisfied with that answer.

AN "EX POST FACTO" EXPERIMENT.

Sec 16.—Nearly forty years since I purchased an old worn-out farm, three miles South of Palmyra, of fifty acres of land, known as Indian Hill. The soil was sandy, old, worn-out, poor The former occupant obtained a scanty subsistence for his family. I plowed and sowed thirty-five acres of winter wheat; the first crop paid for the farm, at 70 cents per bushel I occupied this place seven years, and during this time paid for 158 acres of land, all joined, built house, barn, &c, &c.

THE SECRET OF SUCCESS.

Sec 17 —Through poverty, penury, and want, after plowing the ground, I took two light poles, notched the ends together, put in a cross piece , with two inch auger bored holes, with smaller auger for teeth, made the teeth of wood, and in two hours' time had a drag all complete ; the drag when finished a man of common strength could carry half a mile with ease

Sec 18 —This drag, in leveling my land before sowing, I put a weight upon, and after leveling (a thing I always did), I removed the weight from the drag, and it would run on the surface of this yellow sand, while the points of the teeth did not enter the sand to exceed a half inch

Gentle reader, during the seven years, from first to last, I used this drag or a similar one, and to the astonishment of all, myself included, I never raised a crop of grain on that farm that yielded less than twenty bushels to the acre

Sec 19 —This farm lies in the north part of Ontario County, in the State of New York, and in the town of Manchester In 1832, I removed to Michigan, borrowed a large heavy drag and nearly lost two or three crops, so ignorant was I of the cause of my success in the State of New York.

Sec. 20 —On coming to Michigan, I brought all the pride of a new comer. Success had always followed my efforts. To

be thus baffled in a new country on the very soil of my own
choosing did not set well ; so, after various hints from my
better half, I concluded to try the wooden drag again, ard made
one with forty teeth, much heavier than formerly, but my land
was new with heavy sod   I succeeded without knowing the
cause. Gentle reader, I kept on succeeding, my land became
mellow and a chance occurred   I took a large drag with long
iron teeth, and dragged a few acres through the middle of a
large field   This did the work both for your humble servant,
and the wheat, and the drag too   I received scarce half a
crop from this strip of land of all lengths of straw   Some
green short heads never did ripen, but the writer of this
did.

CORN.

SEC 21.—Remember the seed grows but one tier of roots
They always grow large and run deep into the ground   The
stock, straw, or body will always grow proportioned to the
root.

SEC 22—If the reader will plant one hill deep and one
hill shallow, and will watch them, he will see the shallow-
planted hill sprout first, and both root and sprout will be
larger and will grow faster, and be ahead of the other, the
whole season, the stalk will be larger, with more joints in the
stalk, it will ripen earlier, with larger ears, and the ears generally filled to the end of the cob   For further description
the reader is referred to experiment No. 1, in Chap. 4, 3d
Sec.   There he will find a full description of how the writer
planted and covered in 1855, and he will here add, follows
the same laws, the same rules here laid down for all crops, and
considers them good enough.

NOTE.

The reader will please take notice that no land is so poor
or worn out that under this system he can not raise good crops
The wheat will grow taller and the heads all of a height and
large, but it is important that the roots of all crops should

have a mellow, well-pulverized soil. The hardest red clay made fine will produce good wheat, and all crops will be materially benefited by following this system

SEC. 23.—One of the most common objections raised to shallow planting or light covering of the seed, consists in the supposition that the earth at seeding time will be dry, and the seed will not sprout or grow The answer is plain It is heat and moisture that sprouts all seeds We frequently have sprouted wheat standing in the field and also in the shock. Did it require cold, moist earth to sprout that wheat ? It is usually known that the heat of the sun dries the top surface down during the day time, and the moisture rises during the night. This usually sprouts all seeds, but, as errors sometimes occur, I take the liberty here to state, that I deem it important that all seeds should be covered so as to protect them from the scorching rays of the sun, still as light as will answer for that purpose I am already asked, is not this a violation of Nature's law? I answer, No. It is not probable that seeds in their primitive state were as prolific as at present; that each seed was not endowed with the same power of production as at present, or that perhaps the scorching rays of an equatorial sun, suffered as many seeds to vegetate and grow as at present. There are some farmers who plant deeper and uncover at hoeing; usually, there is no difficulty I believe the seed is more likely to vegetate near the surface of the ground.

5

CHAPTER 7.

GENERAL REMARKS

The writer feels confident of the truths laid down in the First Chapter of this work, especially on the principle of breaking roots to growing trees, having tried numerous experiments in a variety of ways. He has taken young peach trees, whose wood is very tender, cut a root, and in a few days found the same streaks or symptoms of decay commencing; and while experimenting in the young timber, he has cut a root to a number of trees. Some of these he has let stand, while a number have been cut and split open, exposing the commencement of decay in small poles the whole length, while those standing in each and every case show dead limbs in the top.

Sec. 2—The writer is satisfied that the sap passes through the arteries or grains of timber always up, but never down, that there is something in the formations of the grains or arteries of all timber which prevents it. The sap carries the disease from an injured root the whole length of the tallest tree, but never down that where a tree is severed by the axe. The body will run a little sap immediately adjoining the wound, while the stump, being fed by the roots, will pour it out for weeks

Sec. 3—Let us take a more extensive view of the subject under consideration

A hurricane sweeps through the forest, withing, bending and bowing the timber, racking it from its foundation, up-

turning some, loosening and breaking thousands of roots.
The same black streaks follow these breaks and the effects of
these winds can be seen and known by the dead limbs and
trees in all forests of timber Water at the root, will show
dead wood in the tops first. Wherever a mill pond has been
raised, flowing timber, its effects can be seen in the dead tops
of the trees. Hollow trees originate from the same cause.
The heart becomes rotten, from the break of roots; the rotten
wood falls and leaves the shell.

Sec. 4 —It will be readily inferred from the foregoing
that no injury will accrue to trees from pruning or grafting;
still, the writer thinks extremes, like cutting large limbs, or in
grafting, cutting the whole top at once, should be avoided—
that it will check the flow of sap.

Sec 5 —It will require judgment, scrutiny, perhaps, to
distinguish between the suckers and the main roots of large
trees, or in old orchards. The reader will find the main roots
dwarfed, small and weak, but these suckers should be cut if
the main roots are alive If these suckers have killed the main
roots, then the tree is dead

Sec 6 —That there is a class of trees through the
country unprovided for in this work, is certain. In the examinations of orchards, I have found a few of the class above
mentioned, how extensive they may be, the writer is not informed This class of trees originated from a piece of a root,
with a graft stuck in the end or side, and then set in a nursery
and sold as trees. These possess none of the formations which
constitute a tree, they have no regular set of roots, no seat
of life, and are only a temporary thing, short lived, will not
last long, or grow large They are only a substitute for a tree
and should be avoided by all purchasers The best tree ever
grown, come from the seed, was never removed or plowed.
The roots of a tree are its sheet anchor and should run on top
of the ground, and be protected

Sec. 7.—The system commended to the people is a
retreat from former usage. It places the tree in a state of re-

covery, it does not extract the rotten heart, and supply it with
sound wood. Barren trees will bear fruit under this system,
and I have never witnessed an exception, nor heard it from
others

WHEAT, RYE, OATS, BARLEY, CORN.

Sec 8—From experience I think it safe to say, that
the wheat, oats, rye and barley, and corn crops, will be in-
creased in their products, one-third, by following the directions laid down in this work, and will be of better quality,
with less labor for team at least.

GENERAL REMARKS.

Gentle reader, this work is not an imaginary work, but
practical, written by a farmer for the farmers. It is no
patent right, but founded on Nature's laws which can not be
patented. Does this work contain exaggerations? I think
not, if the reports of the Farmers' Club are in any manner to
be relied on. The disaster to fruits and the orchards of the
whole country must be similar. This scientific body of men,
situated in the great city of New York, have correspondents in every state of the Union, or nearly so. The written
and oral information from these correspondents when-
ever the subject is touched upon, all speak of the sickly,
diseased, and dying state of the fruit trees, and the loss of
the fruits, and very similar reports may be found in any
Agricultural journal through the whole country.

QUOTATIONS FROM THE PRESS

Solon Robinson, one of the members of this Scientific
body, says in the *N Y. Tribune* : "All through the Eastern
States, great pains have been taken They have fertilized,
cultivated, planted new orchards, but so far from finding a
remedy then trees are decaying and dying everywhere, and
seem doomed ," and adds, " this is the most important subject, that can engage the American farmer." G W South-
wick of Madison, Indiana, says : "This is the oldest settled
part of the state and formerly had plenty of apples, but for

the last few years, orchards have uniformly failed" Mr. Peters recommends draining Mr Carpenter says draining will not do, for "I have tried it," and charges it to adverse atmospheric influences and insects Dr J V. C. Smith says "It is old-fashioned industry that has died out," and recommends keeping swine in the orchard Mr. Geddes says "Our orchards in central New York formerly died out, but as we have replanted on other ground we have good crops" Dr Trimble adds, "corn and wheat are dying out, as much as apple trees ; give them fertile soil, and cultivation, and if the East wind hurts them, stop it by building stone walls." S E Todd says pruning trees excessively is very injurious A M Powell, of the *Anti-Slavery Standard*, knows of a successful orchard in Columbia Co , N Y , which himself and father cured by exterminating the borers and caterpillars , cultivated, and seeded down Mr. Quinn adds, "give apple trees the same care you do corn and potatoes, cultivate the same, and they will bear;" says pruning is necessary

In the N Y. *Tribune* of Jan. 27th, Mr. Wolvington of Milton, Pa , asks, "how shall I have plenty of apples?" Daniel Cornell of Buckingham, Iowa, says he planted 12 trees 20 inches deep, 4 years old, which never blossomed and never will J D. Hicks of Blain Co , Indiana, asks of the Club, what he shall do with an old orchard— asks if he had not better cut it down They recommend plowing it thoroughly. A Jackson of Willow Grove, Delaware, says he has planted five orchards in his time Each has borne only 3 or 4 years, and died ; thinks it came from grafting. Another gent says the insects will soon drive us across the Mississippi, and we shall be calling on the Rocky Mountains for fruit

This list of names might be multiplied indefinitely if the subject required it The writer deems the above sufficient to show the distracted state of public opinion as to the cause, and that the destruction does exist, and is extensive

Reader, these extracts are very imperfect and contracted, and only present the glimmerings of an inexpressible gloom

that pervades all classes of fruit growers. These quotations
come through the press and from the representative men of
the oldest, the youngest, and the vast area of country contained in the Central States of the Union   Nearly all unite
in the facts, that the fruit trees and the fruits thereof, are
on the wane, and as the fruit trees increase, the disaster in-
creases All remedies recommended and applied have proved a
fallacy. Under one treatment the tree shows temporary pros-
perity, and then shows it was only a revival before death Go
where we will, we behold the fruit wormy, foul and filthy,
and the tree will present the appearance of a patient in the
last stages of measles or the small pox, showing the pits or
pustules in the bark   Gentle reader, be not deceived; it is
consumption of the tubercular kind; it is death with a temporary resurrection perhaps, for there is no tree so hard to
kill, there is no tree that clings to life with more tenacity
than the apple tree The writer of this does not suppose the
disease of our fruit trees to have sprung from slight visionary or
transient causes, but that the tree has been broken at its foun-
tain, its seat of life, and the disease is real, and no visionary,
temporary prescription will be of any permanent use Its roots
are broken, its feeders are severed   How would a cow feed in
the coral blossoms of clover with her mouth chopped off.
Gentle reader, all natural trees have but one set of roots, and
these roots come out of the body at or near the surface of
the ground You will find a healthy, sound tree largest at the
seat of life. The tree begins to spread several feet high,
and grows larger towards the ground   Do your fruit trees
resemble these trees ? Do the large roots come out of the body
above ground ? are there any large roots in sight ? are there
any roots in sight at all in your apple orchard ? Please com-
pare the natural with the artificial tree, and see which suffers
by comparison. The truth is, the earth to a certain depth
should be filled with roots in all orchards of any age or size,
and these roots should originate from the seed and be protected. The reader will very soon learn that there is
meaning in the word "root," and that any damage done to the

root will, soon show itself. The writer has taken some trouble to find what was going on in the Horticultural world, and finds no change recommended, while the calamities seem to be on the increase ; the same old track and practice is weekly, daily, and monthly recommended by all the agricultural papers You behold the fruit growers setting new orchards on the same old plan, you see him filling the places made vacant in his old orchard by cultivation, you see him sorting his fruits for the market, you see his family clinging to their fruit with all that is filial and affectionate, while the scrubby trees, clothed in the yellow and sable garments of decay and death, present a ghastly appearance.

In examinations made in wheat, I have generally found the length of a straw shortened according to the depth the seed was covered The deeper the seed was covered the shorter and finer the straw would be, and this rule seemed to apply to the length of the head Corn also presents the same appearance.

I find also that if the seed of a stalk of corn, three or four inches high, be broken off, or detached, the stalk will not produce an ear of corn Many seeds of different kinds detached from the plant at a certain age will not produce ; others will depreciate in quality. I think this is the cause of chess in wheat

I will now present a most singular witness bearing upon the truths laid down in this work. The witness is Dr Halleck of the American Institute Farmers' Club. The quotation is taken from the *N. Y Tribune* of Nov. 25, 1868, and is in the following words :

" The apple tree, as we know, is artificial, and its fruit is artificial. In its natural state it bears fruit the same as the oak bears acorns Taking it from its natural state, it is subject to influences we do not understand There is certainly a decrease of the apple crop in the Hudson river country. J. W Staples, Newburg, Orange Co, N. Y, asks the Club if the leaves turning brown and falling off, will injure the fruit ? The Chair stated of course, if the leaves perish the fruit must. Dr. Trimble says it is probably caused by the long rains,

and then adds, ' but this is only a confession of our ignorance.'"

These quotations come from two substantial members of
the Farmers' Club—the seat of scientific discussion and examination on all subjects connected with fruit trees or their
fruits They tell us these questions are not well understood,
that they remain a mystery unsolved The next most natural
question would arise, where shall we go for information ?
The writer would most respectfully invite all who have or
ever expect to have any interest in fruit trees, to go to the
roots of your trees for the information, cut a root and in a
short time it will answer the question, and solve the problem
to the entire satisfaction of all concerned

Notwithstanding the writer in the fore part of this work
excluded all root crops, still, and nevertheless, if eventually, it
should be established, demonstrated and proved that the potato rot, decline and decay, has come from our universal
system of hilling, then most assuredly the fault will not be
chargeable to the writer For, suppose the multitude of
small roots emanating from the vine above the seed should
cause a diseased vine, this of course would account for the
numerous insects and bugs found among the vines and stand
charged and indicted by many writers as guilty of the whole
destruction As the writer needs more evidence he submits
the question

GENERAL REMARKS.

Farmers, from the extracts just submitted it is evident
that our fruit trees are decaying and dying everywhere and
are doomed And as their fruits are growing less in quantity
and more foul in quality, we behold our improved acres in-
creasing, while our crops are diminishing in an alarming de-
gree, according to the statistics of the Agricultural Bureau
at Washington ; and, when we ask for information respecting
the cause or causes of the decline, we are informed of our
simplicity. If we call for investigation, we are reminded of our
ignorance If we grasp the pen with a view of inquiry we
are informed our composition is bad, our language is vulgar.

The author expects no exemption from these general charges, but demands a fair trial of the principles laid down in this work, and is willing to trust the result. The writer does not claim to be the original discoverer of all the parts and pieces contained in this abridgement, but has gathered, experimented, and tried them Some he has improved upon, while others he has rejected as worthless The most important parts he has hastily endeavoured to condense and present to the people

NOTE:—If the reader should fail to believe that the first cause of rust on wheat comes from the souring of the milk contained in the berry, please to bite the kernel

6

THE PROTEST

The Fruit Trees protested, both the Peach and the Plum
" Our bodies are rotten, from our bark oozes gum
Our roots are all broken, and plowed like a fallow—
Thus banked and thus buried we can but be hollow '

The Apple Tree spoke, as though it felt some like fighting
" I have stood all the frosts, the thunder and lightning—
You plowed off my roots, and called it no sin,
So eat wormy Apples and pick out the skins !"

The Wheat then came forward, as it was said,
And cried to the people ' I furnish you bread'
By the laws of my nature, and laws of my birth,
My seed used to fall on *top* of the earth !"

The Oats and the Barley both spoke without fear
" Our grain feeds your horses, the barley makes beer
If you cover our seed so that it *can't spread*,
It will grow but *one straw and a very short head !"*

The Corn spoke at last, and thus spoke to the Wheat
" You boast of your bread—don't I make the meat?
With two tiers of roots my slim stalks they will bend—
I will give you *green ears, with a cob at the end"*

AND SO THE END

DARIUS PEIRCE

42

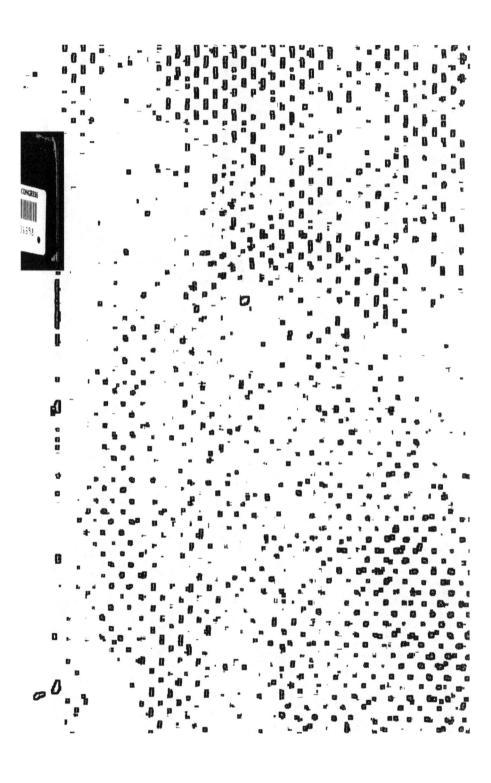

CPSIA information can be obtained
at www.ICGtesting.com
Printed in the USA
BVHW03*1112220518
517007BV00007B/49/P

9 781363 653843